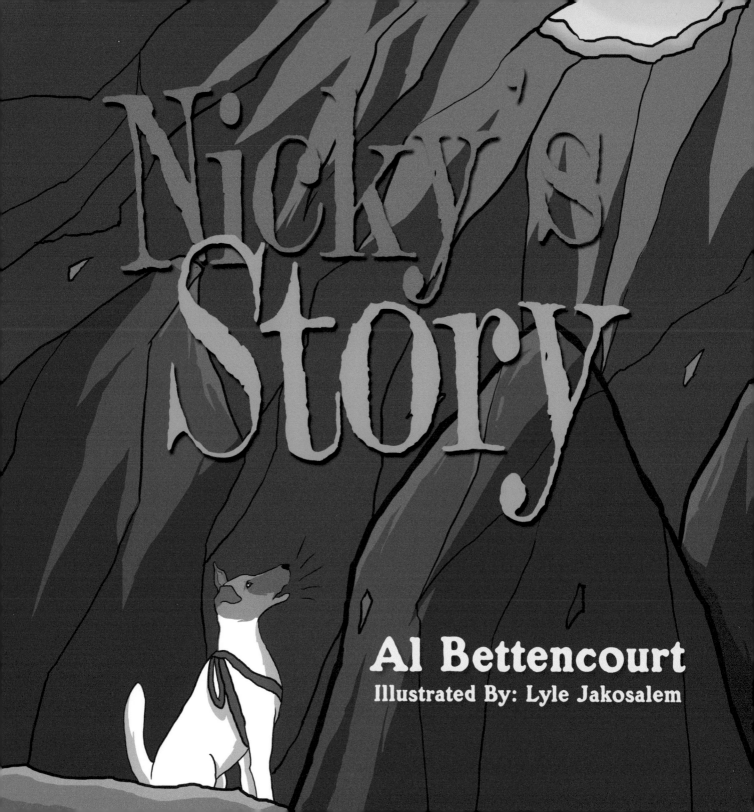

Print information available on the last page

Rev. date: 04/21/2016

To order additional copies of this book, contact:
Xlibris
1-888-795-4274
www.Xlibris.com
Orders@Xlibris.com

NICKY'S STORY

Al Bettencourt

Illustrated By:Lyle Jakosalem

NICKY'S STORY

They say cats have nine lives. Well, I am going to tell you a story about an incredible little doggy that seemed to have many lives!

My wife, Gail, got Nicky from the local animal shelter. When she heard that they had a young fox terrier, she said that it was the dog that she wanted to see. It was mutual love at first sight.

Nicky had been found running around outside the shelter. He had been taped into a box with duct tape and placed on the steps overnight before he managed to get out. The people at the shelter did not know Nicky's name or age, but they estimated he was about one year old. Since it was Christmas, Gail decided to call him "Nick," which was short for St. Nicholas. "Nick" soon turned into "Nicky."

When I first met Nicky, he barked at me. It seemed that he didn't like men. Gail and I often wondered if his previous owner had been a man who had mistreated him. Nicky had a damaged ear that had healed, but he could never extend it like he could the other ear. However, after I spent some time with him, he and I became great pals.

We had different nicknames for Nicky. Gail liked to call him "Niki-nu" and I called him "Nick-mice-ta." Nicky's elegant long nose reminded me of a cartoon character I had seen years ago, the maestro of an orchestra whose long chin extended into the air.

Nicky was a fox terrier, a breed bred to hunt small animals. He loved to chase squirrels. He would chase them up to the invisible fence where he would be greeted with a shock.

Fox terriers also liked to bounce. Whenever we took him out, Nicky would jump straight up and down and bounce at the door. He loved playing with a ball.

Nicky was a very high-strung dog and liked to bark a lot. Gail had to give him some intensive training to calm him down. He slept with Gail and me in our bed every night. He loved it when Gail gave him a massage. He would roll over on his back with his legs up until Gail would accommodate him.

He hated to be left alone, so we took him with us everywhere we could. He would bark at the car window to make us put it down, and he would stick his head out to feel the breeze. When we had to go away for long periods, we would put him in a kennel. Many years ago the kennel owner had a fox terrier and he loved Nicky and Nicky loved him. When we would pick Nicky up from the kennel, he would run up to us with his tail wagging and bark with joy all the way home. Nicky loved to be with other dogs, and many times my daughter would bring over her dog, Snuggles (a beagle), to play with him.

One night it was very windy. I was in the finished basement watching TV. Gail had gone to bed on the second floor. When I went to bed, I saw that the wind had blown the door open on the first floor. I went upstairs and asked Gail where Nicky was. She did not know. We guessed that he had run outside, and we raced out to find him.

We searched and searched but could not find him. The next morning we called all the animal shelters to ask if he was there. We also asked the shelters to be on the lookout for him. We put an ad in the *Providence Journal* and put posters up all over the neighborhood. There was a golf course next to where we lived, and the owner took Gail all over the course in a golf cart to try to find Nicky, but we still could not find him. We thought the worst. Had he been attacked by coyotes? After a couple of days we had lost all hope. It was a very sad time.

But in the middle of the afternoon, three days after the incident, there was a knock on the door. Somehow I knew someone was bringing news about Nicky. Sure enough, a neighbor told me there was a little dog trapped in a hole, but he wasn't sure if it was ours.

"Is he alive?" I asked.

"I don't know," said the man.

We all went to see. There were several people kneeling on the ground, looking down a sink hole. They called out and warned us that only one of us should go to the hole out of fear that too much weight might make the ground collapse. I approached where they were. Firemen and a woman from the animal shelter were already hard at work rescuing the dog. They had a long pole and a flashlight. I looked into the hole and there was our Nicky, twelve feet down in the ground. And best of all, he was alive!

Fortunately, Gail had put a harness on Nicky; it was what we used when we walked him during the day. The fireman kept trying to hook Nicky's harness with the pole, but he was not having much luck. What would we do if he couldn't hook him? We couldn't dig him out; those big boulders might fall on him. Also, the hole was very big, so we couldn't always see where Nicky was.

They asked me to call him, hoping the sound of my voice would keep Nicky from wandering off into the shadows. I called to him and Nicky barked back! It was a faint bark, but a bark nevertheless. All of a sudden, the fireman said, "Got him!" He had hooked the harness and started pulling Nicky up. My eyes filled with tears as Nicky got closer and closer to the top of the hole. But there was a twist in the hole, and the fireman was having a hard time pulling Nicky through it. Nicky yelped at one point, but the fireman still pulled him up. Soon after, Nicky was on the ground and stood up! He looked tired, but he looked okay.

They put a rope on his harness and the woman said to me, "You can walk him into the house or you can carry him."

"I'll carry him" I said, and I took Nicky into my arms and walked to Gail, who was delighted to see him. Gail stayed behind for another minute, thanking all the people who had rescued him.

It's a good thing Gail paid closer attention to what the staff member from the animal shelter said. She had mentioned to me that he was probably dehydrated, so I carried him into the house and started to give him some water. Gail came in and said, "No, Al, we can't give him water; it might hurt him. We have to take him to the hospital to get hydrated properly." Nicky had only taken a couple of licks of water before I took the bowl away from him. We took him to the hospital, where he spent the night getting rehydrated. The next day we went and picked him up. He came out of the back room with the vet, his tail wagging. We had our doggy back!

To show the animal shelter staff just how grateful we were for their help in bringing Nicky safely home, we went to the shelter and made a donation.

It was such a pleasure having Nicky back with us. He was his old self and showed no signs of having been stuck in a hole for three days. We went back to giving him his walks, and Gail went back to giving him his massages. He was back in bed with us.

But about one week after the trauma, Nicky endured yet another calamity. When I was at a business meeting, Gail took Nicky out for a walk. A little boy with two large dogs approached Nicky and Gail. The dogs decided they did not like Nicky and attacked him. His leash wrapped around Gail's legs, and in the confusion, she was almost knocked to the ground. Gail yelled for help, and after what seemed like an eternity, the dogs' owner came out and got the dogs under control—but the damage had been done.

Gail took Nicky inside and let him rest for a moment, but then she noticed he was bleeding. The dog's owner came over to see how he was. Gail said she had to take him to the animal hospital. The dog's owner and her little boy, who had been walking the big dogs, went with Gail to the animal hospital. Gail called me and asked me to come.

"Why?" I asked "What's the matter?"

"It's a long story," Gail said.

I wasn't at the animal hospital long before we got the bad news from the vet. Nicky needed fifty stitches and several drains on his body to release fluids. He would also have to stay in the hospital for several days. We went into the back room to say good night to him, and he really didn't want us to leave him there. He barked and barked. As hard as it was to hear his cries, we knew we had to leave him there. We visited him every day until we finally got to take him home. It took a while, but he healed.

Sometimes when Gail had to go on errands, I would take Nicky to work with me so he would not be alone. Nicky did not like the UPS men who made deliveries to the office. He would bark at them every time they came. I would have to make sure Nicky was in another room when I saw the UPS guy come up the driveway.

While it seemed Nicky didn't like men when he first met them, it was not the same with women. He absolutely loved my secretary from the start. He liked everyone after he got to trust them, and he was a very lovable dog.

One day when I brought Nicky to the office, I opened up the car door to let Nicky out just as a big truck pulled into the parking lot. Nicky bolted out the door and charged after the truck. I grabbed for his leash, but Nicky was too fast. Fortunately, the driver saw him coming and slammed on the breaks. The front of the back wheel touched Nicky but the truck stopped. If the driver had not seen him, Nicky would have been run over.

Nicky *hated* the John Deere lawnmower Gail used to mow the lawn. One day it was broken and a mechanic and I were working on it. I had tied Nicky up with his leash. We repaired the mower, and I took it for a test drive. All of a sudden, out of nowhere, Nicky came charging after the lawn mower and was biting the front tire!

I was used to driving my big tractor, but I did not drive the John Deere very much. On the big tractor, the pedal that allows you to stop it is on the right, but on the John Deere, the right pedal makes you go faster. So at first instead of slowing down, I went faster and ran over Nicky with the front wheel of the tractor! Nicky's leash went under the mower, which was going round and round, but Nicky got up and charged the mower again, and at the same time his leash was caught by the mower, pulling him in. I finally realized I was on the John Deere and stopped it by releasing my right foot from the pedal, but the front wheel was right on top of Nicky. All this happen in a period of about five seconds.

The mechanic and I lifted the tractor off Nicky. I thought for sure he would have broken bones. I felt Nicky for injuries and miraculously, he seemed okay. I let him go and guess what he did? He charged after the John Deere, which was now stopped, and bit at the tires! What a feisty little guy he was!

When Nicky was about thirteen years old, he got very sick. He looked at Gail as if to say, "Did you think I was going to stay with you forever?" Gail and I decided to send Nicky away to doggy paradise, and that is where he resides today safe and sound. We put a plaque up in the backyard, which we call Nicky's Field.

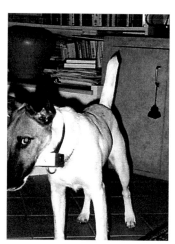

Nicky's Field
Dedicated to a Marvelous Dog

Nicky
AKA
Nick
Nickynu
Nickmaester
Nicholas

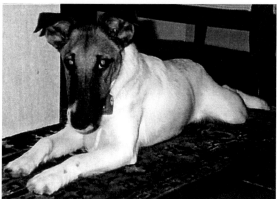

Printed in the United States
By Bookmasters